Recollections of
a Moorland Lad

Recollections of
a Moorland Lad

Richard Robinson

First published in Great Britain by Merlin Unwin Books, 2016

Merlin Unwin Books
Palmers House
7 Corve Street
Ludlow
Shropshire SY8 1DB
U.K.

www.merlinunwin.co.uk

Designed and set in Warnock Pro by Merlin Unwin
Printed and bound by Melita Press

ISBN 978-1-910723-23-4

Contents

Looking west from Drinkwaters Farm at the foot of Great Hill, towards White Coppice, during the winter.

Acknowledgements

It was summer 2015 when I read again these written memoirs of my Grandfather. For many years they had lain in a box in my desk and without the help of a Withnell resident and friend, David Fairclough, they could still be lying there.

I am indebted to him for giving freely of his time, for typing, and for his computer and photographic knowledge in restoring some of the old photographs in the book. Also for those photographs taken and loaned by himself.

Thank you to Margaret Sturrock, Susan Sheppard, Dorothy Boyle, Vera Briggs, David Knight, Joyce Frost, Alan Holden and Kenneth Fazackerley for photographs loaned, and also to the owners of certain photographs reproduced in this book whom I have been unable to trace, despite having made every reasonable effort to do so.

I also record here my gratitude to the staff of Blackburn Museum, Blackburn Reference Library, County Records Office Preston and Ian Lynch of Lynch Antiques, Feniscowles. Finally, thank you to Karen, Merlin and the staff of Merlin Unwin Books for their encouragement and advice and for bringing this book into publication.

Author's Note

The stories I am about to relate are mostly from my own observations and many are closely connected with myself and my own experiences. I can vouch for the truth of them all. Now let me tell them in my own way.

Richard Robinson
Thornlea House
Brinscall
6 December 1957

About the Author

RICHARD ROBINSON was born in 1883 and was brought up by his Grandparents at Botany Bay Farm on Withnell Moors. At the age of eleven he was working half-time and by thirteen he was fully employed as an apprentice stonemason. Most of the work was done in the surrounding villages but he also worked on Blackburn Cathedral and Darwen Tower.

In 1902 he enlisted in the Kings Shropshire Light Infantry Regiment and in 1906 he married Annie Roberts and had two daughters, Martha and Marian.

He was the oldest of six brothers who all saw active service in the 1914-1918 war. Being wounded, he was discharged with the rank of Regimental Sergeant Major. After the war he became secretary to the local branch of ex-servicemen and in connection with this he worked tirelessly on their behalf. On the home guard being formed in 1940, he joined as instructor to the local platoon but had to retire due to long hours of work. He was still working at the age of 73, engaged in building the two vestries and the porch for St. Paul's Church, Withnell.

He was a local historian. His favourite occupations were writing, reading and the natural history of the moorlands which he loved.

He died 12 June 1963 aged 79 at his home in Brinscall.

The Robinson family, friends and neighbours assembled outside Summer House (the correct name of this farm is Botany Bay Farm). The circled child is thought to be Richard Robinson. The farmhouse was built about 1805, around about the time of the industrial revolution when thousands of people were being transported to Botany Bay, Australia for

trivial offences. As it was on the bleak moorlands, people said that anyone living there was as good as transported, hence its name. The stone over the window bearing the inscription 'H.B.H. 1843' should never have been placed there. Its origin was Hollinshead Hall and the inscription H.B.H. represents Henry Brock-Hollinshead.

All that remained of Botany Bay Farm on Withnell Moor in the 1960s where Richard Robinson and his family lived for the first nineteen years of his life, when he left to join the King's Shropshire Light Infantry Regiment.
The old beech tree behind is still standing today, a sad remnant of its former glory over 100 years ago.

Introduction

by Barbara Butler
Grand-daughter of Richard Robinson

If you ramble on the many worn tracks and footpaths of Withnell Moors, take time to imagine what it was like to live there some 120-130 years ago in one of the farmsteads that dotted the landscape, now with few exceptions all sadly reduced to piles of moss-covered stones. Each of these farms and cottages once stood in its own enclosure of stone walls, green pastures and meadows.

Botany Bay Farm (or Summer House as it was known locally) was one of these moorland farms where Richard Robinson – my grandfather – lived for the first nineteen years of his life from 1883-1902. He was educated at St. Paul's Elementary School, Withnell, long since taken down. It stood where the road to Fellstone Vale branches off Bury Lane.

After being at school for a year he could read and write quite well. Recalling taking home his first book and sitting

13

by the turf fire, the farm work done, he began to read aloud. 'My grandfather stared at me in astonishment. It seemed to be beyond his understanding that I could read while he himself couldn't read his own name, never having attended school.' (compulsory education for all finally became law in 1880).

In the 1950s Richard Robinson wrote down his memories of a Withnell Moors childhood. It is best that you read these stories as they have been written down by himself, some sixty or so years ago, after his retirement as a stone mason. I hope you will enjoy reading them.

Barbara Butler

August 2016
Withnell

Chapter One

My School Days 1889-1896

Living with my grandparents at the Summer House were three cousins of mine, all boys and all older than myself. It was the custom in those days for boys to smoke twist tobacco in clay pipes. My three cousins had already learned the wiles of my lady nicotine: no boy was considered a 'man' if he couldn't smoke before he went 'half time' which meant a half day at school and the other half day at work. They went 'half time' at ten years old in those days.

At St Paul's school then, the schoolmaster's name was Briggs. He had a rough handful with the boys, but he left in 1885 and for a time the school was in the sole charge of the assistant schoolmistress, by name Miss Dinah Hull; the boys now got almost completely out of control and it became quite common for the boys to 'light up' their pipes in school. They paid school money in those days but much of that money never reached the school as there were too many sweet and tobacco shops by the way.

In the schoolroom there was a gallery of tiers which started from the floor and was complete with seats and desks on every tier; sometimes when a boy was very unruly he was put under this gallery minus his clogs. Many of the boys carried long pins in the seams of their coats; some of these seats had knot holes in them and woe be to any scholar who was sitting over one of these knot holes.

One scholar named Harry was very unruly and was always 'getting the stick'. He put his wits to work: he carried a large live frog to school in his coat pocket and when Miss Hull offered to go near him to cane him, he would pull the frog from his pocket and hold it in front of him by its back legs so that she dare not go near him. Harry is still living in Alberta, Canada, and is around the eighty mark.

My cousin Dick was also very unruly and one day when Miss Hull had caned him he called her 'a b***** asker and a brid neesin' b****r'. Newts were known as askers then, and of course 'brid neesin' was bird nesting; why he called her these names I do not know!

Classroom in St Paul's School, Withnell. Desks and seats arranged in tiers this way so that the pupils had a good view of the blackboard and teacher – and no doubt, the teacher of them, possibly Miss Dinah Hull standing on the left.

Every self-respecting schoolboy smoked one!

On my first day in school in 1889 I was taken there by my three cousins, all smoking clay pipes. When we reached the top of 'Owd Ike's Broo' (Norcross Brow) we were joined by six other boys on their way to school, their names were Harry, Jack, Tom, Bill, Hugh and Job, they were all smoking too. In my mind's eye I can still see them as they walked down the 'Broo'.

By this time another schoolmaster had been appointed by the name Mr Tom Pollard. He was a gentleman in every sense of the word. He was a strict disciplinarian, severe yet kindly withal. He demanded from all his scholars' strict obedience, truthfulness, honesty, respect and patriotism and he set the standard by his own example.

He soon put an end to all the nonsense of smoking and swearing and now the boys dare not carry their pipes or tobacco to school for he would often make them turn out their pockets. As they dare not now carry their pipes to school they used to hide them in the old stone wall at the bottom of 'Owd Ike's Broo'. About thirty years ago, when the road was being widened, that old stone wall was pulled down. I worked on it and we found many old clay pipes and what looked like little pieces of rope. My workmates couldn't understand how they came to be there, but I knew. I enlightened them.

SCHOOLBOY AND SCHOOLGIRL GAMES

Let me give you a brief description of the games we played in those olden days. First, marbles. This was a boy's game and savoured of gambling. Marbles had many rules and phases, and as these differed in different districts there is not room in these memoirs to give them all, so I will content myself with just giving the value of the different kinds of marbles and some of the words used in the game. The coloured marbles made of burnt clay were valued at one; small white ones with

Spinning tops
These tops were often 'chalked' by the children in many different colours making patterns as they spun around.

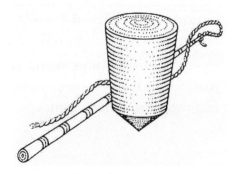

Above: the whips were made of string attached to a wooden stick.

two blue rings round them were valued at two; a glass alley with a spiral of many colours running through the centre was valued at three; the taw which the player flirted between his forefinger and thumb was valued at four. If it had a red or blue vein running through it, it was called a blood alley and was valued at five or six. The words generally used were Foots, that's where the game started from. Clench, corrons, chuck, fudging and 'Ah'l set thi throo'. There was also a game of marbles called Knuckle Hoyle.

There was whip and top. The top was a small round piece of wood with a steel tip. You spun it round with the fingers and then kept it spinning by hitting it with a whip. Then there was another kind of top shaped like a pear with a tip about an inch long. You did not use a whip with this kind of top; the method was to wrap a piece of string round it then taking it in your hand you gave a sharp jerk with a sweep of the arm as you threw it towards the ground, at the same time giving the string a sharp jerk backwards.

These peg tops would spin for a considerable time, particularly if they were spinning on a flag[stone]. There were many experts at these games.

Some of the other games played were: thrust, leap-frog, weep, piggy, cricket, football, rounders and duckstone. To play the latter and get the most fun out of it, you needed five or more players. This was the method: a flat stone was placed on the ground, each player had some stones about the size of a cricket ball (a pebble about that size from a brook was an ideal duckstone). A mark was made on the ground about four yards from the flat stone – this was called the foots as in marbles – then each player threw his stone towards the flat stone, trying to get as near to it as he could, the one farthest away was 'it'. He placed his duck on the flat stone and the other players threw their ducks at it, trying to knock it off. If no-one knocked it off, each player had to go and stand by his duck. The idea was to pick it up and run back to the foots to have another throw.

Once you touched your duck you had to run and if the player who was 'it' tigged you before you reached the foots then you had to take your time at being 'it'. If one of the players succeeded in knocking the duck off the stone then the cry would go up 'Thi duck's off'. The player who was 'it' was not allowed to tig another player unless his duck was on the stone. While his duck was off, all the other players ran back to the foots, and so the game went on.

The girl's games included hopscotch and jacks, but their main game was the skipping rope. The two girls

Skipping, accompanied by an appropriate chant.

that were turning the rope would chant 'pee, po, py, pepper' and at the word pepper they would turn the rope as fast as they could, all the girls would then join in skipping the rope and the chant would then start, 'When I grow up who shall I marry? Tinker, tailor, soldier, sailor, rich-man, poor-man, beggar-man, thief.' Where a girl missed the skip that was the person whom she would marry. Sometimes the boys would join the girls in this game. Yes, they were happy days.

MY FIRST VISIT TO BLACKBURN

My grandparents used to go to Blackburn to 'buy in' their groceries, sometimes on a Wednesday and sometimes on a Saturday. They always went in the old horse and cart. I was four years old when I went with them on my first visit. I can still remember the shop in Victoria Street: the shopkeeper's name was Hayhurst. I must have been very observant even in those days, this is the report I gave on returning, according to my aunts:

I had seen 'Hawses runnin' away wi'heauses' these were the old horse trams. I had also seen 'winda's on t' top o' pows' – these were the street lamps.

Blackburn's Old Market Place, with Victoria Street in the background.

Another early memory

I can remember a girl named Alice Barnes being murdered at Witton Park, Blackburn, in 1892 and a man named Cross Duckworth was later hanged for the crime in Liverpool.

An old horse-drawn tram. Two horses were needed to pull the coach up some of Blackburn's steeper hills. The picture shows a tram at Billinge End Road in Blackburn, about 1888. An extra horse was needed to help with pulling the tram up Montague Street, a very steep Blackburn street.

When I was nine years old I had never tried to smoke and I was getting on towards half time, so now was my chance to learn. It was on a Wednesday during the summer holidays. My grandparents had gone to Blackburn and I was left to take care of the farm while they were away. I knew where my grandfather kept his tobacco and pipes in the buttery. I found them. There were two kinds of tobacco, twist and Cavendish cake, and I decided to try both. I took a pipe and broke the stem off in the approved fashion, then I cut up some of the tobacco as I had often seen my grandfather do, then I rubbed it into shreds and filled my pipe. I need not say what happened; you will know. I must have enjoyed it so much and smoked enough to last me for some time because I did not venture to smoke again until I turned twenty-one.

St Paul's School, Withnell, around 1900. It was built in 1874 and here Richard Robinson began his school days in 1889 at the age of six. Sadly it was demolished in the late 1960s to make way for a modern housing estate: Fellstone Vale.

Botany Bay Farmhouse on Withnell Moor where the author lived as a child. This watercolour shows the farm in the 1950s. By that time it had been partially taken down, including most of the out-buildings and the barn.

CHAPTER TWO

Trial by Jury

We lived at a little isolated farm house on Withnell moors. In the summertime, often on a Sunday morning, several neighbouring farmers and traders from the village would come as far as our house for a walk and a 'camp'. I will give their names here: Joe, Tom, Dick, Billy, Nick and Gabriel.

The first discussion was generally farming; and this disposed of, the affairs of the nation had to be put right. They were all Tories, my grandfather included, except 'Owd Dick', who was a liberal. The debate often became heated. On this particular Sunday morning it became very much so. 'Owd Dick' was in danger of being overwhelmed, he fought back valiantly, but he was fast losing ground.

Suddenly he almost floored the opposition, literally, by asking 'Wod dud Billy Gladstooan say i' 1884?' This rendered the opposition speechless for a time, then one of them asked:

'Why, wod dud he say?' to which 'Owd Dick' retorted 'Aye, wod dud he say?' That was about as far as the argument got for I do not think that any of them knew what 'Billy Gladstooan said in 1884 or at any other time.

The political situation now being ended, there was quiet for a little while, then one of them said 'Led's see, Dick, tha's bin' sittin' on t' Jury at Preston sessions this wick, hesn't ta?'

'Ah hev,' replied Dick.

'Wod is id like sittin' on a jury, Dick?' asked another. 'Wor ta nod feeart?'

'Ther's nowt to be feeart on,' replied Dick. There was a general chorus: 'Tell us o' abaht id!'

'O reet,' said Dick 'Id's as easy as tumblin' off a flittin. O' as tha hes to do is tek nooatis o' t' judge then tha'll nod gooa far wrang, bud ah'll tell yo' just wod happent to me. Ah wer't last to ged theer, thad wer o' Wedensday. As soon as ah landed, a mon wi' a wig on coom to us an' towd us to follo' 'im; he led us i' t' court room an' pud us i' two pews, six in oather, then he sed as we'd hev to sweer, well, tha knows, me belongin' to t' little chapel ah dudn't like thad idea, bud ah soon fun aht as he dudn't meeon cossin'.

'He gied us a little book a peece an' towd us to say summat after 'im, then they o' sterted to mumble sooa ah mumbled wi' 'em. Then he sed as we'd hev to point a fooarmon, ther' wer' a skoomaister among us so we made 'im t' fooarmon. Then t' judge coom in, he hed a wig on too, then another mon wi' a wig on sed 'co t' fost prizner. A woman coom i' dock just at t' front on us. T' mon wi a wig on towd her her name, then he sed as hoo wer charged wi' fell onny, ah duddn'd know what fell onny wor sooa ah axed skoolmaister, he sed hoo'd bin steylin.

'Then t' mon wi' a wig on axed her if hoo wer gilty or nod gilty. Hoo sed 'nod gilty' bud onnybody wi' a pair o' een i' ther head could see as hoo wer. Then another woman coom i' another box, hoo sed ass hoo kept a shop, an' this other woman hed come to her shop an' axed her if hoo wod give her summat, hoo said as hoo'd nowt to spare, then t' other woman sterted to gooa aht o' t' shop, when hoo wer passin' a table hoo took a looaf off a table at side at t' dooer an' pud id under her shawl, hoo followed her aht an' towd a pleecemon. Then t' pleecemon went i' t' box, he sed when t' shop woman towd 'im as t' woman hed tekken a looaf he followed her, hoo hed a looaf under her shawl, when he axed her where hoo'd getten id hoo towd 'im to mind his own business, sooa he locked her up.

'Then another mon wi' a wig on geet up an' axed t' pleecemon a too a thri questions, then he torned tort us, he sed as he wer pleased to see so monny intelligent faces among us, he sed as id wor a sad case, this woman wer a widda wi' four little childer an' they hed nowt to eat for three days, t'womans husband hed bin deead four yers an' left her wi' four little childer to bring up, hoo hed to pop o' her things, when hoo'd popped 'em o' hoo hed to torn aht to wark, then hoo sterted to be ill an' hor an her childer hed nowt left, hoo went to this shop to see if hoo could cadge owt, when t' shop woman towd her as hoo'd nowt to spare hoo set off aht o' t' shop, as hoo wer passin' a table hoo seed some loaves on't table, hoo thowt o' her little childer an hoo couldn'd abide to see 'em sterve sooa hoo pud one o' them loaves under her shawl, t' poor woman dudn't know wod hoo wer doing, he sed as hoo wer more to be pitied than blamed.

'Gentlemen,' he sed 'those four little childer are waiting at hooam fer ther mother, ah ax yo' to send her back to 'em.' Then he seet dahn.

'Then t' judge towd us o' abaht id, he sed as id wer a sad case, bud being poor wer no excuse for steylin', hoo could a gone to t' union. Ah dudn'd know wod he ment bi t' union sooa ah axed t' skoomaister, he sed as hoo'd bin' steylin' an' t' union ment warkheause. Then t' judge axed t' woman why hoo hedn'd bin to t' union; hoo sed as hoo'd bin theer, bud they towd her as they couldn'd do nowt for her unless hoo went inside wi' her childer. Hoo sed as hoo couldn't do thad. Then t' judge axed us to give a verdick. Wi fon her gilty baht leeovin t' box an t' judge sed as ther hed bin a lot o' steylin' lately an' he'd hev to mek an example on her, an' he gied her six months wi' herd labour.

'Well, thad's abaht o' ther is to id, i' those three days wi tried twenty seven on 'em, ah never thowt as ther wer so monny scamps i' t' country. Wi fon 'em o' gilty. O' t' other cases wer summat same 'cept one, we had to leeov t' box to decide his case, he'd bin steylin', he sed as he wer nod gilty bud it wer as plain as a pikestaff as he wor, when we geet to t' little room skoomaister axed us wod wer eaur views on id; mooast on em wanted to find him nod gilty, an' they wod a done bod for me, they sterted to argue wi' me, bud ah sed 'Nah, chaps, just use a bit of common sense, wod hes t' pleece browt him here for if he's nod gilty?' Thad settled it, they'd never thowt abaht thad. We went back an' fon him gilty an t' judge gied him a month i' jail.

'Bud t' last case wer' t' best, this mon hed bin steylin' eggs aht o' a hen coyt, he warned satisfied wi' thad, he wer tekkin' th' hens as laid 'em too, fermer catched him red honded an' handed 'im o'er to t' pleece. He coom in't prizners box, as soon as ah clapt mi een on 'im ah could see as he wer gilty. When he wer axed if he wer gilty or nod gilty he sed as he wer nod gilty. Ah nelly brasted aht o' laffin, id wer eosy to see as he wer gilty, his clooas wer i' rags, he'd no collar nor tie on, his hair wer o' ruffled an' he dudn't look like as he'd hed a wesh or a shave fer a month.

'We fon him gilty baht leeovin' t' box an' t' judge gied him twelve months. Thad ended id. Ah've no complaint to mek cept as ah hed to pay mi own expenses, an wasted three days an geet nowt for id. Bud ther's one thing as tha lerns on a jury an thad is ther's no country i' t' warld where a mon geds as fair a trial as he does i' this country.'

However much the company had disagreed with 'Owd Dick' on politics, they were all in entire agreement with his last statement. It was now dinnertime and they left to go home for another week.

That was 64 years ago. All those simple yet honest old men have, long ago, appeared before the Great Judge of all; whether he *'fon 'em o' gilty as soon as he clapt his een on 'em'* we may know some day.

When they had all gone, I carefully considered 'Owd Dick's' version of sitting on a jury, and I made up my mind there and then that if I ever had to appear in the dock before a jury, particularly if the jury was composed of men like 'Old Dick' I would do my best to appear in a brand new suit, nicely creased and pressed, a clean collar and tie, my hair and teeth nicely brushed, and clean washed and shaved. I thought that if I could only do that I should stand a good chance, whatever my offence, of being acquitted without a stain on my character, but I hoped that might never happen.

Alas, all my hopes were dashed to the ground, for before the year was out, I, a Moorland Lad, stood in the dock. It happened in this way...

Chapter Three

My own Brush with the Law

As we lived at an isolated farmhouse, and as I had plenty of work to do when I came home from school, it was very rare that I got down in the village except on a Saturday. My spending money in those days was usually a ha'penny, on odd occasions a penny, but often nothing. It was the first week in November and the day Saturday. As I had been a good lad that week, my grandmother gave me a penny.

After tea I did my work on the farm and about seven-o-clock I sauntered down to the village, where I met two of my schoolmates, Granville and Hugh. Gran had a penny and Hugh a ha'penny. We put our store of wealth together, then the question arose: how should we spend it? Should we buy a ha'poth of chips each and spend the other penny on fireworks? Or should we go the whole hog and spend the whole lot to celebrate the time-honoured occasion? We went in conference, no banking house of Messrs Rothschild ever discussed a financial problem more minutely or seriously. At last it was put to the vote and chips won: three for, none against. We went to the chip shop, it was a little wooden hut in Railway Road in those days. After our sumptuous repast we came out. 'Come the four corners of the world in arms, and we shall shock them,' seemed to be our attitude.

We went to a newsagents shop, another wooden hut a few doors away. This shop sold fireworks and we stood for a time looking at the fireworks in the window: there were canons ½d each, pin wheels, flip flaps, sparklers etc. two for a a'penny. There were also bundles of squibs, which we called Russian guns. These were little red cardboard cylinders, about an inch long and about half as thick as an ordinary lead pencil, all tied together by their fuses at the top in bundles of thirty, two bundles a penny. Gran went in and bought two bundles. We divided them under the shop window.

We then walked to the top of Railway Road, with Church Brow (Bury Lane) on our left and 'Owd Ike's Brow' on our right. We went up 'Ike's Brow' which was a narrow old sandy lane in those days; a brook ran down one side, there were no houses there then, all was quiet there, the usual traffic down that brow would be about three farmer's carts a week. As we crept up that brow, Robert Catesby, Guido Fawkes and all their fellow conspirators could have taught us nothing.

When we got about halfway up, we commenced our

work. The first one was fired off and it made about as much noise as when you clap your hands together. By blowing our breath on the pieces of the first one, you could get a glow sufficient to light the other fuses from it. We had got about half way through our task when suddenly out of the gloom and the shade of the wall we saw a figure rushing towards us, it had a helmet on its head and a row of bright buttons in front of its coat. Did we run? Yes, but the policeman caught Hugh, and he told all our names.

On the Monday the policeman came to the school and the schoolmaster called us out and took us to meet him in a little classroom. The policeman asked us all our correct

Railway Road, also called Station Road, Brinscall.

35

names and addresses and he said we would be reported. We went back to our classes. Nearly three weeks passed and as we had heard nothing further we began to think that we had been let off, but that was not so.

On the Saturday morning the policeman came to our farm house. I was not at home so he offered the summons to my aunt. 'No,' she said 'Ah'm nod hevvin' id, ah've nod bin summunzed'. The policeman waited until I returned then served it on the real culprit, myself. I opened it, it was blue in colour and about sixteen inches long and ten inches wide. It was a fearsome looking document.

Bury Lane, Withnell. Behind the high stone wall on the right stands the Marriage & Pinnocks Mill and the road climbing up from the bottom of Bury Lane is Norcross Brow (Owd Ike's Broo). And behind the trees lie the Withnell Moors.

It was headed:

COUNTY PALATINE OF LANCASTER

Then the Royal Arms complete with a Lion and Unicorn then:

PETTY SESSIONAL DIVISION OF LEYLAND

Next my name and address, then it read something like this:

TAKE NOTICE
Information has been laid before me this day by George Norris of Chorley, Superintendent of Police, for that you on a certain date did unlawfully let off certain fireworks on a certain highway in Withnell. You are therefore hereby summoned to appear before a Court of Summary Jurisdiction to be holden in the court house, St Thomas's Road, Chorley, in the county aforesaid, at half past ten-o-clock in the forenoon to answer to the said charge.
On Tuesday the _ _ _ day of December 1893

signed _ _ _ _ _ _ _ _ _ _ _ _ _ _
Magistrate

We duly appeared, but there were only myself and Gran. Evidently Hugh had turned Queen's Evidence. When our names were called, two policemen shepherded us into the dock. We could not see over the top so two stools were brought for us to stand on. We pleaded 'Guilty'.

Then the policeman went into the witness box. He said he was proceeding along in the normal course of his duty when he heard several loud explosions. On going to ascertain the cause, he found myself and Gran letting off fireworks. He was a man about six feet tall and about fifteen stone. I thought I heard a few titters in court and the magistrate smiled as he told how he crept up the wall side until he got near us, then he rushed out at us and succeeded in catching one of us.

When he had finished his evidence, the smile vanished from the magistrate's face. He looked at us very severely over the top of his spectacles. He said he was surprised to see that two small boys like us had begun to tread the downward path at such a tender age. We had already embarked on a life of crime, but luckily for us we had been caught in time and checked and he hoped it would be a lesson to us. He said it was his duty to see that peaceful citizens were not terrorised by a gang of hooligans.

He could only do this in one way, and that was by inflicting severe penalties, therefore we should each be fined 1/- and costs.

The total cost was 7/- each.

That was the first and last time I was called upon to appear before a court of law. Whether, in the cause of justice, I ought to have done so I must leave you to guess, and the future is in the lap of the gods.

As in the case of Trial by Jury, the magistrate, policeman, my two schoolmates and all the others connected with the case have gone to rest. I am the only one left. I hope they were all dealt with as we were on that memorable occasion. I have no grievance with them, they were but doing their duty according to their lights in those 'Good Old Days'.

Church Brow (Bury Lane), off Railway Road, circa 1930.

The Withnell Moors ruin in the foreground is Solomon's Temple farmhouse. Darwen Tower sits atop the hill on the horizon.

Chapter Four

The Withnell Moorlands

Between Withnell in the north, Belmont in the south, Darwen in the east and Horwich in the west, there is a vast expanse of wild moorland where the curlew, lapwing and grouse are the sole occupants. Here one may wander a whole day without meeting a single soul. But it was not always so; I can remember a time when more than a hundred farmhouses and cottages dotted these moorlands here and there. Here in these stone buildings with stone flagged floors, the people lived, and although they were rough, yet kind hearts were dwelling there; penury demanded from them incessant toil which was given ungrudgingly.

Where now are the mills and workshops where the people earned an honest livelihood? The little cotton mill in Tockholes was demolished in 1904; this mill was a three

Brinscall Hall Calico Print Works. Owned by the Christopher Woods of Brinscall Hall, now little remains of its existence. The large warehouse, Woodside Cottages and stables, just off centre of the picture at Shop Fold also belonged to the Print Works. The horses stabled here were used to cart the logwood from Brinscall Station to Brinscall Mill. Logwood being used to produce a dye for the Print Works.

storeyed building with a weaving shed attached, taping, warping, winding and weaving were carried on here and employed over one hundred people who lived in the old numerous cottages that surrounded the mill.

There was also an inn there but now only a few houses remain. To generate the steam to drive the engine, coal was mined from the outcrops in the Darwen hills. These are the legendary Tockholes treacle mines. The mill and its tall chimney was a landmark for miles but now only a few scattered stones mark the place where it once stood.

Just below the mill stood Garstang Hall which was demolished in 1906. In 1910 the then-vicar of Tockholes, the Rev AT Corfield begged some of these stones from the Liverpool corporation, and using them, myself and an old friend of mine, Mr J Paley of Withnell, built the Norman arch that is over the well built in the wall of the vicarage by the roadside. We also built the outdoor pulpit that stands by the old Tockholes schoolhouse just inside the lych gate. Just by this pulpit there stands an old sun dial, [the old stone plinth is still there, minus the inscripted plate] now covered with verdigris; on its face there are numerous inscriptions. One I remember quite well is:

> *'Contemplate when the sun declines,*
> *Thy death with due reflection;*
> *And when again he rising shines,*
> *The day of resurrection.'*

In 1912 myself and Mr Paley demolished the last part of the old Hollinshead Hall. It was wintertime and one day there came a very heavy snow-storm, we spent that night in a little building

The pulpit at St Stephen's Church, Tockholes.
This pulpit was built with stone from Garstang [Garstanes]
Hall, which was situated close by the old Tockholes Cotton
Mill. In this churchyard also is the grave of John Osbaldeston,
1780-1862, the inventor of the Weft Fork. This invention
would stop the power-loom when the weft threads snapped.
It made lots of money for the mill owners, but poor John died
in poverty.

– still preserved – containing an ancient old wishing well.

At Brinscall, the print works, the little bleaching croft, the blue brick works and the mill known as Marriage & Pinnocks have all disappeared. These found work for more than a thousand people. Only the tall chimney at the printworks now stands. [since demolished]

Now little evidence remains of what once were busy hives of industry where all the people round about earned an honest livelihood. The click of the engine, the hurrying clogs of the workers, the rattle of the looms, and the sound of various whistles calling work-people to their work are all now silent, and have gone forever.

A song I knew as a boy can perhaps describe the scene better than I can myself and it is for that reason that I give it here.

Ben Bolt

'Oh, don't you remember sweet Alice, Ben Bolt?
Sweet Alice with eyes so brown,
She wept with delight when you gave her a smile
And trembled with fear at your frown.
In the old churchyard in the valley, Ben Bolt,
In a corner obscure and alone,
They have fitted a slab of granite so grey,
And sweet Alice lies under the stone.

Oh don't you remember the wood, Ben Bolt?
On the green sunny slope of the hill,
Where we sat and sang together, Ben Bolt,
And kept time to the click of the mill.
Now the mill has gone to decay Ben Bolt,
And a quiet now reigns all around,
See, the old rustic porch with its roses so sweet,
Lies scattered and fallen to the ground.

Oh don't you remember the school Ben Bolt,
And the master so kind and so true.
And the dear little nook by the clear running brook,
Where we gathered the flowers as they grew.
On the master's grave grows the grass, Ben Bolt,
And the running little brook is now dry,
And of all the friends who were schoolmates then,
There remains Ben but you and I.

And where now are all the farmsteads and cottages that dotted the moorlands, where on special occasions the farming people would foregather, make merry and dance and sing until well into the morning-side to the latest tunes of the times? All have gone, only a few scattered stones mark the place where once they stood, and in some cases there is no trace left at all. When I wander among these ruins I can in some cases say for certain where each building stood. I can say 'The porch was here, the kitchen there, the shippon here and the stable there but in some cases I am not now so sure and I can only say '

They stood somewhere about here'. I knew all the people who dwelt there and although they are invisible yet I seem to feel their presence very near. Yes, mills, workshops, farmsteads and cottages all have gone, and: 'A quiet now reigns all around.'

Customs and trades

There were many old customs and trades in the olden days that are now long forgotten. The old farmhouses on the moors were lit up with oil lamps or tallow candles. These candles needed to be 'snuffed' every now and then. Wax candles were a luxury. The fires were mostly of turf or peat.

From the old Solomon's Temple farmhouse, right along the moors to Piccadilly on the main Preston to Bolton road, there is a peat 'breast' ranging from three to eight feet in depth. In the summer time this was cut up with a hay knife in small pieces about a foot square and three inches thick, these pieces were put to dry on the moorland, then carted to the farmhouses and stacked ready for use in the winter time. But it had other uses: during the last two decades of the nineteenth century, hundreds of tons were carted to Samlesbury paper mill to be used in the manufacture of brown wrapping paper.

When walking across these moors about sixty years ago, one might have seen a man pulling up the heather. This was an old besom maker known all around as 'Owd Besom Harry'. When Harry had pulled up sufficient heather to satisfy his immediate needs, he would spread it out to dry in the sun to 'season'. When it was ready, he would tie it in bundles and carry them to an old derelict farm house which he had made his workshop. Often when I was going home from school I would help him to carry them, for which he would reward me with an a'penny, and on odd occasions, with a penny.

HARRY THE BESOM-SELLER

Most of the farmers on these moors made their own besoms with which they swept out their farm buildings, but Harry made them for sale. As he was a master craftsman at this work, his besoms were in great demand. One little printing works at Belmont used them almost exclusively to sweep out their buildings and yards: their usual order was for sixteen dozen at a time. When Harry got this usual order he would come across here to our house to see if my old grandfather would cart them for him – no one else was ever entrusted with this particular journey for reasons you will learn. By the way, my grandfather was known as 'Owd Jemmy'.

On the Monday morning Owd Jemmy would 'gear up' his horse and cart and make his way towards Harry's workshop. As man and horse jogged along shoulder to shoulder through the heather, they seemed to be part of the moorland itself, so well did they fit into the moorland scene.

By noon they would have loaded up the cart and then they would set out on their journey, This they always did in stages. The first stage ended at the *Hare & Hounds Inn* at Abbey Village, about one and a half miles away. On arriving there the horse would be taken to the stable, fed and watered, then Harry and Jemmy would go to the kitchen for refreshments: so ended the first stage. On the Tuesday morning they would be up betimes and away on the second stage, which ended at *Piccadilly*, a little inn about two miles further up the road. The Wednesday morning would see them off once more on the last stage of the outward journey.

On arriving at the works they would unload the besoms and get paid for them, which, I believe was half a crown a dozen. Then they would adjourn to the *Black Dog* a little inn that nestles at the foot of the moorlands at the bottom of the valley in Belmont village. Unloading besoms was a very thirsty and arduous task, for they 'ganged' no further that day. On the Thursday morning they would set out on the first stage of the return journey, which, as before ended at *Piccadilly*.

On the Friday they would complete the second stage of the return journey and would stay once again at the *Hare & Hounds*. They would arrive home about tea time on the Saturday. To complete the whole journey of about five miles each way, a full week had gone by and so had the besom money. These old people have been laid to rest now these many years, and their faults lie lightly on them. With the passing of 'Owd Harry' there probably passed the last of these besom makers from these parts of the moorlands.

BACON CURING AND BUTTER-MAKING

When we killed pigs we used to cure the sides of bacon. Often my hands have been sore with rubbing the salt into them. And I have spent hundreds of hours making butter in the old 'up and down' churn.

My grandmother used to make black puddings and I have never tasted any others to equal them. In Blackburn, vendors used to carry black puddings around in a can heated by hot water. They frequented the inns and public houses.

In those days there used to stand on the boulevard, a potato boiler, something like a miniature Stephenson's Rocket, there you could buy a penno'th a potatoes and salt and eat them as you walked along. These were still around in the late 1940s.

Many of the old farmhouses would have had their own butter churns

Now back to the old farmhouses. These were visited each week by all kinds of traders and vendors with their wares. There were travellers in suits, underclothing, socks, stockings and other kinds of drapery: these were called 'Scotchmen'. They carried their wares strapped on their backs. Where the ITV transmitting station now stands on Winter Hill, there is a memorial which

Right: Scotchman's stump marks the place of the murdered travelling draper

Below: Watercolour of Scotchman's Lane, behind the Butterworth Brow cottages

states that a 'Scotchman' was murdered there and robbed of half a crown. I believe his name was Henderson.

TRIPE AND TRADERS

Other traders came round with tripe, trotters and cow heels, cockles, mussels, fresh fish and red herrings. I have not tasted the latter delicacy for more than forty years. Some carried tea, coffee and cocoa, some needles, thread, pins, wool, buttons and other useful articles. There were traders and craftsmen, scissor and knife grinders and saw sharpeners, tub hoopers, cane and rush bottom chair menders. Then there was the lamp oil man, who also sold salt in blocks which you could crush with a rolling pin, as well as sand which was sprinkled on flag floors to keep them clean. It certainly kept the flags clean, but covered everything else in dust!

BEESWAX AND BAKING

Every Saturday all the furniture was polished with bees wax and turpentine until you could see to shave yourself in them. Fenders, toubars, fire tongs and pokers were scoured with sand or emery paper until they shone like silver. All the bread, barm cakes and other cakes were baked in the old fashioned ovens. I have carried many scores of flour, barm and carbonate of soda to that old farmhouse for this purpose, but it was worth it: there is no bread like it today.

In passing, I must mention a few pieces of furniture we had. First, there was a Singer sewing machine, one of the first that that company ever made; it was working up to a few years ago, but something broke and couldn't be replaced. Second, there was an old oak gate-legged table, black with age, and when it was opened it was a perfect circle, six feet in diameter, round which a dozen people could sit in comfort. Third, an old clock made entirely of oak: all the wheels, axles, barrels, pins, the face and fingers were of wood and all cut and carved by hand, even the weights were of wood. The only things about it that were not made of wood were the cords. What became of that old clock I do not know, but it was an antique then.

A typical farmhouse range. These ranges were made by companies like Carron of Falkirk and would often advertise the retailers shop name into the metalwork across the front of the range or on a fixed metal plate eg 'Booth of Preston' or Baldwin, Blackburn.

AMUSEMENTS AND ENTERTAINMENTS

In those days we made most of our entertainment ourselves, but there were traders who travelled round the little villages with their wares, these traders would often have singing contests and other similar diversions. One of these I remember was a family called Parsons, who had four sisters, all good singers. One of them had a deep bass voice and could sing *Asleep in the Deep* and similar songs along with the best. In later years they appeared several times on the Blackburn Palace variety stage. Then there were the village fairs with swings, roundabouts etc; and the annual school tea parties and concerts.

HOUSE PARTIES

Here in the old house [Botany Bay Farmhouse/Summer House] many parties and revels have taken place, parties of weavers, winders, etc used to come from the mills round about and sometimes from as far as Bolton, Blackburn, and Preston. We used to boil our own hams and make teas for them in the summertime and we always kept a cask of ale and bottles of spirits for them to enjoy.

They usually arrived about teatime on the Saturday afternoon. After tea they would either play games in the meadow or ramble off in little groups in different directions and eventually would put in an appearance again at dusk. After a little supper, the tables would be put away and the floor cleared for dancing, with the music provided either from a concertina, melodian or mouth organ. How their eyes would sparkle as they waltzed around to the tunes of the times: *After the Ball, Daisy Bell, Two Little Girls in Blue, I'll be your Sweetheart, Little Annie Rooney, Comrades* and many others I can still recall to mind. In between the dances they would take their turns in singing these old songs, the whole company coming in on the chorus.

The dancing and singing would continue well into the morningside,then they would get rest as best they could. Many stayed on that day following till after tea, when they would finally depart. These parties took place throughout the summer months on most fine weekends.

When winter came with its frost and snow, the old house was very quiet until the end of the year. There were then two special nights reserved for family gatherings: Christmas Eve and New Year's Eve.

On Christmas Eve all the family, their friends and sweethearts would foregather in the old kitchen. At eight o' clock they would enjoy a traditional Christmas supper, then the room would be cleared for dancing and singing, songs of the times, dancing of old and carols which took place one after another until past midnight.

On New Year's Eve the company would again foregather, but this evening would be on a more lively note. After the usual festive tea the floor would again be cleared. The first item called for a song. There were four Atkinson sisters present, all grand singers. Agnes would oblige with the first song, *The Bailiff's Daughter of Islington* then Maggie and Polly would follow with a duet and Nellie would sing a school song, then we would dance 'The Lancers'. After this strenuous dance, further singing would take place. Joe Tootal would sing Steven Foster's lovely song *Beautiful Dreamer* and for an encore *Down by the Old Mill Stream*. But Joe had another song, *Master and Man*, he was a fine singer and I have no doubt but that, had he taken his songs on the variety stage, he would have been hailed a 'Star'. The next dance would be a Polka, then further songs.

Fred Butterfield would entertain the company with several songs, one I remember went something like this:

'I wish I was a squire, an MP or an Earl , and blow me if I wouldn't marry old Brown's girl.'

For an encore he would sing a song of which I do not know the title, but well remember the theme of the song; it was about an amorous parson who was in the habit of kissing the cook but at the house where this took place they had a parrot and when it saw the kissing it would say, 'I can see thee, I can see thee.' To keep the parrot from seeing, they placed a large jampot in front of the parrot's cage:

'Then the parrot in the cage, went in an awful rage,
The parson took the cook upon his knee,
She kissed him once or twice, said the parson 'this is nice'
And the Parrot shouted 'jam, jam, jam.'"

There would then be a waltz, more singing and so the fun would go on, fast and furious, until the finger of the old clock would be climbing uphill towards midnight. A few minutes before twelve there would be a request for the old song, *The Miner's Dream of Home*. Fred Butterfield would come out and with his back to the fire he would begin:

'It's ten weary years since I left England's shore,
In a far distant country to roam,
How I longed to return to my own native land,
Back to the old folks at home.
Last night as I slumbered I had a strange dream,
One that seemed to bring distant friends near,
I dreamt of old England, the land of my birth,
To the memory of her sons ever dear,
And I saw the old homestead, and faces I loved
saw England's valleys and dells,
And I listened with joy, as I did when a boy,
To the sound of the old village bells.
The log was burning brightly, twas a night that should
Banish all sin,
For the bells were ringing the old year out
And the New Year in.'

The chorus would then be sung again by all. Ah! Dear old Fred, I can still see you now in my mind's eye, you are still with us and should this meet your eye, may it bring back many happy memories of those olden days, now long past.

As the old clock struck twelve all the company would stand and with hands joined together the musicians and singers would all join in:

'Should auld acquaintance be forgot'
An ' never brought to mind?
Should auld acquaintance be forgot,
An' days o' auld Lang Syne?'

Then the glasses would be filled and Joe Tootal would give a toast:

'Here's a happy and prosperous New Year to everybody, wherever they may be.'

The fun would then continue until the time came to part. My mind often wanders back to those olden days and times when all seemed young.

Jack Higgins, world champion jumper

About this time the world champion and famous jumper, Jack Higgins, was in his hey-day. His feats are well known. We had a horse just seventeen hands high and he jumped over this with ease on the bowling green at the Royal Hotel in Abbey Village. He did most of his training in Abbey Village, and his trainer's name was Jack Marchant.

Among his trick jumping was to jump on a basket of eggs and off again without breaking any. A man could lie down and Higgins would jump on his face and off without hurting him – he would also jump on a bowl of water and off again without sinking. One enthusiastic spectator thought he would try the latter at home.

In the back yard where he lived was a large tub sunk level with the ground and full of water; he tried on this, he managed to jump on the water alright but failed to rise again, and went to the bottom. No, he wasn't drowned, as the tub was not very deep.

A young apprentice clog maker lived in Abbey Village at that time and he made all Higgins's clogs for him. He also went round with Higgins and his trainer. One day after training they were going home and they came to a five barred gate.

Jack Higgins, a mill worker who became a famous jumper. His astounding feats of jumping were known worldwide. He would jump over the canal in Blackburn, skimming the water in the middle before landing on the other side. It is said that at the age of 55 he could still jump over a horse and cab with ease.

Brinscall clog and shoe makers, Bert Guest and son.

Higgins walked up to it with his hands in his pockets and went over it with ease; this caused his trainer to remark 'Higgins, thar't laziest devil ah've ever seen, afooar tha'll tek thi hands aht o' thi pocket an' oppen t' gate tha'll jump o'er id'. That clog maker is still making clogs and we often talk about Jack Higgins and his jumping.

CLOGS AND PIGEONS

In those days clogs were the general footwear in Lancashire. Clogs were a work of art: they were often narrow toed and had two or three rows of brass nails round the toes, the two sides where the clasps were had several rows of eyelets in various colours, and the fronts had all kinds of patterns cut in them. Most boys in those days kept pigeons and pigeon-keeping was known as 'The Fancy'. They would often have pigeon races and the usual dress for those in 'The Fancy' was a pair of fancy clogs, a silk scarf or muffler round their necks and a cloth cap worn on one side of their head.

In Darwen was what was known as the 'Trading Hoyle', at the weekends the 'fanciers' would carry their pigeons to Darwen and do a trade, walking there and back and if they had made threepence on the day's dealing, they had had a good day.

A gentleman who lived in Wheelton, Mr Ernest Jackson, had a loft specially built for racing pigeons. Once when he lost some of his pigeons he came round the district to see if anyone there had 'stragged' them. One man to whom

Workday clogs. These were the general footwear in the mills, worn by both men and women.

he went said he hadn't got them: 'Tha con come an' look i' my loft,' he said. His 'loft' consisted of an orange box.

One day a cat paid a visit to this 'loft' and carried off several pigeons. The owner of the 'loft' caught the cat and decided to drown it. He filled a large earthenware mug with water, put the cat in and then put a sack over it, but the cat kept putting its head out, he got a hammer to hit it on the head with, but he 'skenned' and missed the cat and so instead hit the mug and broke it into pieces; he got wet through and the cat ran away. He didn't catch the cat again. Yes, those days were not without their humorous side.

CHAPTER FIVE

I Start Work

Just before I was ten years old, the age that one could go 'Half Time' [half school, half work] was raised to eleven. I went to work at that age. I started work at Marriage & Pinnocks cotton mill, learning to weave. This was a job I never liked. Oft on dark winter mornings I have run over a mile on Withnell moorlands through snowdrifts, snow, rain, hail, sleet, wind or fog to be at the mill by 6am, and oft have I been 'clouted' for being a few minutes late and many times I have dried my clothes on my back.

I started 'tenting' in what was called the new shed. It was the first place to be lit up with electricity in Withnell. Eventually I was put on two looms. The average earnings per loom were five and sixpence; twenty two shilling for a four-loom weaver and eleven shillings for two. I never

Marriage & Pinnocks Mill at Withnell – the cotton spinning and weaving mill where my grandfather, the author of this book, started work at the age of 11.

reached that average; my work was bad and I was often fined for making poor work. Sometimes it was so bad that I had to buy the cloth. There was never so much cloth in that old farmhouse either before or since.

In those days there was what was known as the 'slate system'. After booking up each week, the tackler would come round to each weaver with a large slate, and you had to tell him how many pieces of different sorts you had woven during the week. As the tacklers wage was on a poundage of what his weavers earned, any weaver who had not reached the 'average' was abused with swear words by the tackler.

I was sworn at every week. I eventually got the sack. Those were the good old days.

Drawing-in frames at Marriage & Pinnocks Mill in the 1890s.

Workers at the Withnell Mill.

My Next Job

The question was now: what was to be done with me? My father was a stonemason, and at that time he and a fellow mason named Harry Flew were engaged on building Darwen Tower. I was sent there. Yes, I helped to build Darwen Tower, and I am probably the only one left now who worked on that tower!

My father and Harry Flew both lived in Wheelton and they walked to the tower and back each day. They had to set out before five in the morning so as to be at work by seven-o-clock; they worked until half past five at night and then walked home again. They both liked a 'pint'.

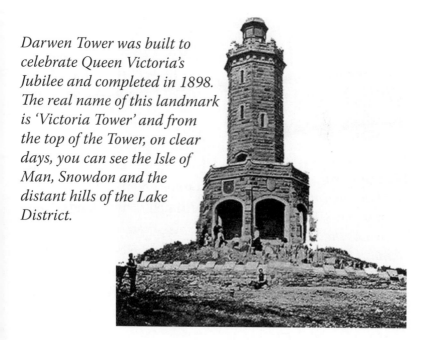

Darwen Tower was built to celebrate Queen Victoria's Jubilee and completed in 1898. The real name of this landmark is 'Victoria Tower' and from the top of the Tower, on clear days, you can see the Isle of Man, Snowdon and the distant hills of the Lake District.

One day they went down to the *Sunnyhurst Hotel* and the landlord asked them why they didn't lodge nearer their work instead of walking all that way, to which Harry replied 'Oh we can't do that, you see we have a little gardening to do when we get home'

My next job was at Hoghton Tower. When you walk along the road just below Hoghton church you will see that the carriage drive goes straight from the road to the tower. Previously that carriage drive only went as far as the lodge half way up the hill; from there it wound to the left and went in a roundabout way to the tower. It was in 1898 that the road was cut straight to the tower.

The Withnell Brickworks, built in 1898
Built at the time of the Gold Rush in 1898, it was locally known as the Klondike, the name of the river where gold was prospected in the Yukon region of North West Canada.

Withnell brickworks was built in 1898 also, it was called Klondike, because it was built in the same year as the gold rush to the Klondike.

Also in 1898, Mr W.B. Parke who owned Abbey Mill and all the houses round about and also the Withnell moorlands and farms thereon, decided to sell the whole lot. Abbey Mill and the farms and houses around it were sold to Mr William Birtwistle and the

Abbey Village Methodist School. This photo of the pupils was taken in the mid-1890s. The pupil standing left, back row, is Robert Moss, born at Pickerings Farm in the 1880s. His father, John Moss, was gamekeeper to Mr Parke, landowner of the Withnell Moors at that time. The moors were sold, along with all the farms and cottages, to Liverpool Corporation in 1898. In 1936 the school was badly damaged by fire and the school was out of action for about one year. The pupils were then taught in the Methodist Chapel.

Withnell moorlands, the farms and cottages to the Liverpool Corporation. Mr Birtwistle decided to do away with the old fashioned mule spinning and instead install ring spinning. Some of the mule spinners were sacked. The others who remained went on strike. Mule spinners were sent from Mr Birtwistle's mills in Blackburn.

This was resented in Abbey Village. They were law abiding and didn't cause any disturbance, but their trade unions engaged a band and this band met the 'blacklegs' at Withnell station every morning and played them up to the mill to the tunes of *Britons Never Shall Be Slaves, Poor old Joe, Ah'm a poor old spinner* etc. and played them back to the station again in the evening. In the end Mr Birtwistle won and the spinners became reconciled to their fate.

Work and Play

About this time, entertainments and amusements were stepped up a little. The popular songs then were: *Daisy Bell, Comrades, At Trinity Church I Met my Doom, For old Time's sake, Two Little Girls in Blue, After The Ball, The Sunshine of Paradise Alley, A Bird in a Gilded Cage, Hi, Tiddley Hi Ti To, Keep It Up, Maggie Murphy's Home* etc.

Blackburn Fair was a great attraction, there was Wall's Ghost Show, Tom Thumb, The usual swings, roundabouts etc. But the main attraction was the first 'living pictures' which were known as the 'bioscopes' the main pictures were of people coming out of the mills, and there was great excitement among the viewers when they recognized themselves coming out of the mill gates.

A Gradely Blegburn Prato Pie

There was a new attraction at this fair. The show people generally arrived on the Wednesday night and as soon as the market stalls had been cleared away they set to work, and worked all night and all day on the Thursday to be ready for the opening on the Saturday, there being no work on Good Friday.

The new attraction was a large tent with a wigwam attached. This show consisted of four wild men from Peru. They were billed as the last of the Incas. I remember their names as they appeared on the large coloured posters: Wepton Nomah, Go Won, Go Mohawk and of course Big Chief. Big Chief could scalp one as easy as shelling peas. While one show was closing and another audience filling the tent, Big Chief would sit in his wigwam telling fortunes at tuppence a time. Entrance to the show was also tuppence.

On the Thursday just before noon an old woman presented herself at the entrance to the wigwam. She carried a large blue and white chequered handkerchief with something wrapped up in it resembling a small bucket. A large Inca, complete with tomahawk, was on guard and he barred her entrance.

'Mustn't disturb Big Chief, Big Chief resting,' he said 'Ah want to see him,' replied the old woman. 'Big Chief very angry if disturbed when resting, dangerous to disturb him,' said the Inca.

'Tell him I want to see him,' she persisted. 'Very well then,' said the wild man 'but you do so at your own risk, I will see if Big Chief will see you.' 'Aye, thad's reet lad,' replied the old woman.

'Ah'm his mother, tell him as ah've browt him a gradely Blegburn pie wi' a crust on an' plenty of meyt an' gravy in id.' Big Chief must have been very pleased and the other wild men from Peru must have taken kindly to the new menu, for while the show remained in Blackburn, every morning just before noon the old woman was seen at the entrance to the wigwam carrying a large blue and white chequered handkerchief with something wrapped up in it like a small bucket, and there is a slight suspicion that it contained a gradely Blegburn prato pie wi' a crust on an' plenty o' meyt an' gravy in id.

Theatre Royal Opera House, Blackburn.

1899 AND THE FUN CONTINUES

Entertainments stepped up again in 1899: the Palace Theatre of Varieties was opened. Most of the world-famous artists have appeared on its stage: Harry Lauder, Gracie Fields, Charlie Chaplin, Tom Foy, George Formby senior, Jack Lane, L'Incognita, Marie Lloyd, Alec Hurley, Cinquevalli, Eugene

The Palace Theatre of Varieties at Blackburn.

Stratton, George Hackenschmidt, Yukio Tani and many others. Others I can remember were Little Tich, Dan Leno, Harry Champion, The Great Laffayette, their names are legion. G.H. Elliot, Albert Whelan, Gracie Fields and Bransby Williams are still with us. And what artists they all were! They had to be, for their livelihood depended on the performance they could put over the footlights.

If you wanted excitement you could go to the Prince's Theatre, just behind the Palace, and there you could see drama and melodrama, *The Sign Of The Cross*, *The Face At The Window*, *Mab's Cross*, *The Man In The Iron Mask*, *Sweeney Todd* and *The Murder In The Red Barn* are among many I can remember. If you wanted grand opera you could go to the Theatre Royal and be entertained by the world's most famous opera companies. Yes, those were the days of entertainment.

CHAPTER SIX

The Fight for the Footpaths

The Liverpool Corporation, now having taken possession of their newly-acquired property, attempted to close many footpaths over the moorlands, particularly those running by the reservoirs between Withnell and Tockholes, but the Preservation of Footpaths Societies from Blackburn and Darwen protested.

As this had no effect, they visited the district at the weekends, bringing a band with them, and to appropriate tunes, accompanied by lusty men carrying saws, axes, crow bars, hammers and wire cutters they proceeded to remove the obstacles that had been placed across the footpaths in no uncertain manner. One Saturday the Corporation ordered the watermen and other employees to oppose them and take their names, but when they did so, the lusty men wielded their tools so fiercely that they decided that discretion was the better part of valour and beat a hasty retreat. In the end the Footpath Societies won the battle and the paths are still open.

During the annual mill holidays in August 1899 it was decided to put in a new engine bed at Abbey Mill; this had already been quarried at Hoghton Quarry, just behind the tower. I was an apprentice to stone masoning by then. The contractor's son and myself were sent down to the quarry to mark the courses and to number the stones so that they could be set in the same places when they were conveyed to the mill.

When we got there all the stonemasons and stone dressers were on strike. They met us but when they learned that we had only come to number the stones, they did not interfere with us further. The cause of the strike was that several stone-sawing and stone-dressing machines had just been installed there. Hoghton quarry was the first quarry in Lancashire to install stone-dressing machinery, perhaps the first in England. It looked like the century was going to end as it had begun in an industrial revolution.

These men said that this new machinery was going to do them out of work, but like those at the beginning of the century, they were misguided. In the end they had to bow down to progress. The installation of the stone-dressing machinery was one of the greatest benefits that ever fell to the stonemasons' trade. It prolonged their lives by twenty or thirty years. At that time I knew about twenty or thirty stonemasons and very few of them lived to reach the half century mark, all victims of silicosis. My own father died at the age of forty six while still a young man from that disease.

When we had completed the engine bed we built a new bay to the weaving shed. When the roof was put on, a Blackburn firm came to glaze the windows, and with them came a young man named Bob Crompton. He was about twenty years old and had just commenced playing with the Blackburn Rovers football team. For many years he played as right full back for both the Rovers and England. He was the captain of the Blackburn Rovers team for many years.

Bob Crompton, glazier, and soon to be captain of Blackburn Rovers.

The South African war was now in progress. I well remember the siege of Ladysmith, Kimberly and Mafeking; they were all relieved in turn. When Mafeking was relieved, it was celebrated by a huge bonfire and fireworks display at Witton. I was there.

The popular songs at that time were *Bluebell, The Soldiers of the Queen, Little Dolly Daydream, Lilly of Laguna, The Honeysuckle and the Bee, Sons of the Sea, Goodbye Dolly*

*The corncrake, once a common bird on Withnell Moor
The ventriloquist of the feathered world, its 'Craick,
craick,' call coming first from over there, then over here.
This is accounted for because it can cover the ground at a
remarkable speed when alarmed. This bird is more heard
than seen and sadly no longer abides here in our meadows.*

Grey etc. I can still remember the tunes and all the words of most of the songs I have mentioned in these memoirs, but don't ask me to sing them: I am neither a tenor, bass or baritone. If I was assessing my voice, I should say it was somewhere between a corncrake and the bullfrog, and that reminds me, it is twenty years since I heard the corncrake. In my young days it was a familiar call in the springtime, but mechanised farming has taken its toll and the corncrake is no longer heard in these parts.

Into the Twentieth Century

The year is 1900 and I have now come to the end of my recollections for the last two decades of the nineteenth century. I have many similar memories of the first two decades of the present century but I do not propose to enter them here, except one and that is in connection with World War One.

At the beginning of these memories I mentioned that my old schoolmaster demanded from all his scholars: obedience, respect, truthfulness and patriotism. That training proved its worth in World War One. I do not recall a single schoolmate of mine who did not join up in some branch of the armed forces. How they acquitted themselves is history and they brought to the village every decoration for bravery including the Victoria Cross.

I and a younger brother were at the retreat from Mons in 1914, we both hold the 1914 star and rosette.

Sometimes when I stand and gaze at the war memorial by the council chamber and read the names there, I see the names of many of those old schoolmates of mine who joined in the merry games we played. They are asleep: *'In Flanders Fields where Poppies blow'*

Richard Robinson, author of this book, King's Shropshire Light Infantry Regiment, early 1900s.

Botany Bay Farm, the childhood home of Richard Robinson, which later became a shooting hut with supplies being brought to it by cart, and by the late 1950s was a ruin.

CONCLUSION

A few weeks ago I paid a visit to that old farmhouse of my childhood on Withnell Moors and as I looked up into the branches of the old tree, the words of Robert Burns came to my mind:

> 'Ye 'mind me o' departed joys
> Departed, never to return.'

As I stood in the old farm fold, now overgrown with grass and gazed at the old ruins, memories of my childhood crowded up on me. In fancy I heard someone singing a song that seemed to be written specially for myself on this occasion.

The Old House

Lonely I wander through scenes of my childhood,
it brings back to memory those happy days of yore;
Gone are the old folk, the house stands deserted,
No light in the window, no welcome at the door.

Here's where the children played games in the heather,
Here's where they sailed their wee boats on the burn,
Where are they now? Some are dead, some have wandered,
No more to that home shall these children return.

The house now is lonely, the moorlands deserted,
The children are scattered, the old folk are gone;
Why stand I here like a ghost and a shadow?
'Tis time I was moving, 'tis time I passed on.

Many and varied are the changes that Old Father Time brings about, even in the brief space of one's own lifetime; and so do things pass away and are forgotten like a tale that is told.

81

Above: All that is left of Botany Bay Farm, colloquially known as The Summer House. It was built about 1805, around about the time of the industrial revolution when thousands of people were being transported to Botany Bay, Australia for trivial offences. As it was on the bleak moorlands, people said that anyone living there was as good as transported, hence its name. I lived there during the first nineteen years of my life.

Richard Robinson returned to this site of his boyhood home many decades later and wrote of the scene above:

'And there was the dear old tree which I climbed thousands of time as a boy: when I played around it with my playmates at football, it was one of the goalposts; at cricket it was the wicket; and a swing hung from its branches. How it must have enjoyed our merry games, but the years have sped since then. Most of my playmates have gone to rest, and like myself, this old firend is getting old.'

The author of this book Richard Robinson (above, far right) holding a spirit level against the dressed stone, working as a stone mason on the new porch and vestries at St Paul's Church.

Richard Robinson, Withnell Moors' stone mason.

CHAPTER SEVEN

Withnell and its Churches

Withnell is mainly non-conformist; there are at present [1950s] four Methodist, two Church of England and one Roman Catholic churches. In the district, 'Abby village' has the oldest church, some well-known families, have been stalwarts of this faith for more than a century. It is claimed that the village is so-called because there was once an Abbey there, but there is no evidence to support this. The style of some windows and the architecture of some old buildings at Roddlesworth suggests that at some remote period they were used as places of worship.

There is a Wesleyan church in Bury Lane, and one in School Lane built in 1899. Prior to worshipping there, the Wesleyans worshipped in the chapel now used as the

The Wesleyan Chapel at the bottom of School Lane, Brinscall, can be seen on the left of the picture above.

W.U.D.C. (Withnell Urban District Council) offices. At the bottom of school lane stands a building built in about 1860, which was used by the United Methodists until the 1930s when they joined the Wesleyans. This was afterwards used as an employment exchange, and during WWII it was used as headquarters by the A.R.P. (Air Raid Precautions), with a siren on its roof. Now it is used as a storeroom by the council.

Before worshipping there, the United Methodists used a building just opposite. This building was originally three cottages: they were then used as a reading and recreation room until 1919 when they were taken over by Mr J. Beaver and turned into a picture place. This building is now the Regal cinema. The fourth Methodist chapel is at Withnell fold.

There are two Church of England churches: St. Paul's at the top of Bury Lane and St. Luke's in Quarry Road. St. Paul's celebrated its centenary two years ago.

Its first vicar was the Reverend Daniel Slyman. He was followed the Reverend G.O.Redman. These two vicars held the benefice for almost seventy years. The services at St. Luke's were taken alternately either by a lay reader or a curate. In the late 1890s a dispute arose between the vicar and his curate, as a result of which the curate left and a number of the congregation left with him. For a time they worshipped in the room over the bank in Railway Road, now used as a Liberal Club. About 1906 St. Paul's church was struck by lightning, a great hole was torn in the roof and the

Going to the pictures or 'flicks' was a very popular choice of entertainment for the villagers. This building was originally three cottages before being used as a recreation and reading room, until it was finally converted into the Regal Cinema.

lead flashing on the spire was completely melted away.

The Catholic Church, St Joseph's, is in Bury Lane, almost opposite St. Paul's Church. Prior to worshipping there, the Catholics worshipped in a building by Marriage and Pinnocks mill and before that in the old 'Salt Pie' in School Lane, now pulled down.

About thirty years ago the bell at St. Joseph's went out of action. I, along with other workmen, were sent to

St Paul's Church, Withnell. In this churchyard stands a memorial to Private James Miller, who was awarded the Victoria Cross in the Great War 1914-18. He will have been known to the author of this book. His body lies in the Dartmoor Cemetery, near Becordel on the Somme, France. He was 26 years of age. Members of Private Miller's family still live in the district today (2016).

Salt Pie is the small building behind the tree where the Roman Catholics worshipped before St Joseph's was built.

ascertain the cause. We erected a scaffold on the roof and found that the bearings on one side of the tower had worn away. We had to remove the bell, and after much difficulty we got it on the scaffold.

On the bell an inscription stated that it was presented to St. Joseph's by a church in Ireland. Cast on the bell are the words 'Erin Go Bragh' [Ireland Forever] and a date which I believe was somewhere about 1650. On the hammer or clapper was another inscription, almost worn away. After much scrutiny I made it out – VOX FIDE VIGILATE ET ORATE. I took a copy of it to the Rev. Father Almand, who was the priest then, and he kindly translated it for me as 'A voice calling the faithful to watch and pray'.

St Joseph's Roman Catholic Church.

Another band of worshippers known as the Bethel held meetings in wooden huts – now pulled down – in Railway Road. Over half a century back, a sect known as Christadelphians worshipped in a wooden tent in the grounds of Withnell Villa, now the estate offices of the Liverpool Corporation. This sect rejected infant baptism.

Two well-known Brinscall families belonged to this sect and all their children were baptised there, but not until they had attained their majority. A large slipper bath was used for this purpose. They ceased to worship there in about 1898.

About that time Mr Job Parkinson, the then-owner of Withnell Villa, started a brewery in his grounds. He purchased the tent and its contents. The tent and the bath were then used to store the ingredients used in the brewing of beer. 'How are the mighty fallen.' 'To what base uses.........'

Many are the changes that take place, even in the brief space of one's own life. Withnell is a very recent place compared with its immediate neighbours, particularly Tockholes and Brindle, whose churches date back to the twelfth century.

Richard Robinson, 1951

WALKING DAYS

Villagers walking in the procession along Railway Road. the tall metal girders rising in the background supported the gantrey which ran from the quarry on Butterworth Brow to Brinscall railway sidings.

91

Parish schools' walking days took place annually in June, around Whitsuntide. After walking through the villages, the procession, accompanied by Brinscall and Withnell Fold Brass Bands, headed to the field, offered for the day by a local farmer. There a well-earned rest with coffee and buns was given to the teachers and scholars. Visitors could also enjoy the same, but were only admitted on payment of 3d each (6d if coffee and buns were included). This was recorded in the Parish Magazine of 1896.

Everyone wore their Sunday best clothes and, if they could be afforded, new outfits were often made at home, either on a sewing machine or hand-sewn, for the occasion.

Chapter Eight

Withnell and its Schools

The oldest known school in Withnell was the little old house, until recently, Brinscall Post Office. There is no one living now who remembers it. It is known that there was a school at Abbey Village in 1806. The next-oldest school was a little building that stood close to the footpath, opposite the present Wesleyan chapel, known as the 'Salt Pie'. It was recently demolished. Although it was a Roman Catholic school, scholars of other denominations were taught there.

On the ground floor there were two rooms used as a day school. The other storey was used as a place of worship. There is at least one old gentleman still living who was taught there; my father was also taught there. When this school was closed, the Catholics moved to a little old building that stood at the corner of Withnell mill, just across from where stands

Mr Astley's grocery shop. A flight of stone steps led to the school room. The Catholic school moved from there when St Joseph's was built.

St Paul's School was built and owned by Mr John Parke, who also owned Withnell mill. When he closed the mill down, the school was closed also. The Scholars then had to go to

Left: Brinscall Wesleyan School was built in 1876 and stood at the top of School Lane. It was largely destroyed by a fire in the late 1920s and was re-built on the same site where it is now a Nursery for pre-school children.

Below: The bottom of School Lane. To the left is Railway Road and straight across is Butterworth Brow leading to the Quarry and Withnell Moors.

Hoghton Old School on School House Lane
Not in Hoghton but in Withnell, due to boundary changes in
the 1920s. In his book 'Paul Withnell', AW King writes that
a member of the De Hoghton family of Hoghton Towers was
the benefactor responsible for the building of the school. He
describes it as 'a rectangular building with two large rooms,
one downstairs and the other upstairs, the upper room
being entered by an outside stone stairway'. Each room had
a fireplace and the desks were fixtures against the walls all
round the rooms. The lower room was for the Day School
and also for the women and girls to have a 'sewing night'. It
was last used by a farmer for storing hay before it was finally
taken down after the building of a new school in Withnell.

Heapey School, which stands just above Heapey church. This school was built in 1820. St Paul's School was later re-opened and controlled by the church as a denominational school.

The next school in Brinscall was the building now used by the Urban District Council as offices. It was a Wesleyan school used as a day school during the week and as a place of worship on Sundays. When Brinscall School was built, where the present Methodist school now stands, the scholars moved there. This school was burnt down twenty one years ago, and the following year the present school was built.

There was just one other old school: it was not really in Withnell but in Hoghton. It stood close to the old Withnell

St Paul's School, built by the owner of Withnell Mill

In 1912 the author spent a night here in the old well house at Hollinshead Hall with a fellow workman when they were demolishing the last part of the main house.

vicarage. It was never used as a school in my time; ever since I can remember it, was used as a barn for storing hay. It has been pulled down for many years. I once came across an old gentleman, now dead a great many years, who told me he attended that school as a boy.

Richard Robinson, 1950

CHAPTER NINE

Withnell Moorlands in the 1890s

This can be taken as an accurate record of the Withnell Moorlands as they were in the 1890s. I have taken great care in the making of this record. With the death of William Rossall Isle in November 1962, aged 93 years, I am the only one now left who lived on these moorlands in 1890.

I shall give you the name of each farm or cottage and the names of the people who lived there and any interesting legends or stories connected with them as they appear in these pages.

It will be noticed that a great many of these farmsteads bear the names such as: Watsons, Pickerings, Snapes, Brooks, Barons, Woods, Ramsdens, Pimms etc. It can only be assumed that these farms, when they were built, were not given names but were called after the people who first tenanted them.

As far as the legends are concerned or the superstitions connected with them, I can only say that I have recorded them as they were recorded to me.

The Liverpool Corporation purchased the water rights of these moorlands about 1850 when they built the third reservoir in the Roddlesworth valley, and constructed the Goit from Abbey village to Anglezarke. When this was done, all the houses, farms, etc. could obtain a licence to sell beer for 5/- (shillings) a year on condition that they found lodging accommodation for a number of the workers on the project, e.g. where the row of houses stood at New Ground, one of them was called the 'Flowing Jug'. Goose Green was known as the 'Green Goose'. Similarly in passing, the same thing applied when the railway was made between Blackburn and Chorley, about 1860. The same thing also applied when the Leeds and Liverpool canal was made in the 1790s.

The Liverpool Corporation purchased the Rivington watershed (the Withnell Moorlands) outright in 1898. They dealt with the people who lived there very humanely and kindly. They did not desire that human beings should live on the watershed, but they did not turn any of them off. When they died or left of their own accord, the premises were not re-let but were allowed to stand untenanted until they were pulled down or fell of their own accord. Only a dozen or so now remain.

Goose Green, once known as The Green Goose when licensed to sell beer.

Most of the old ruins can still be seen but in many cases there is no trace that any building ever stood there e.g. the two cottages (Woodfold Cottages) at Abbey Village.

ROADS AND FOOTPATHS

A great many of the roads and footpaths shown on the map *(see pages 98-99)* were but occupation roads and many footpaths were but paths from one farm to another and in no way can be claimed as a right of way.

BROOKS AND WATER COURSES

In the olden days, before the advent of the motors, there were many wells by the wayside and wherever a brook crosses the road and the road was fenced and the brook ran under the road,

101

a small stile or opening had to be left so that a team master could always get a bucket of water for his team of horses. Many of these still remain. They were jealously guarded as a right. All these moor lands are dotted with streams and wells, many of which never run dry, even in the severest droughts.

HUNDREDS

On the main Preston to Bolton road about two miles from the *Hare and Hounds Inn* and nearer Bolton, there is Calf Hey Bridge. This is the boundary, an arrow carved over the centre of where the brook runs. On the Bolton side is the inscription 'Sharples – Hundred of Salford'. Sharples has now been taken over by the Turton Urban District Council. On the Preston side is the inscription 'Withnell – Hundred of Leyland'.

Many years ago, certainly before 1300AD, all the country was divided into Hundreds. In many parts of the country they are known as Wapentakes. Each was supposed to contain one hundred hides of land, support one hundred families and supply one hundred soldiers for the King. They were ruled over by Barons who also appointed Lords of the Manor. Lords of the Manor tried all trivial cases of offence but the Barons always presided at the Hundreds courts to try serious offences. All these courts were abolished in 1867 when Magistrates' Courts or petty sessional courts were instituted in their place.

WITHNELL

Over the centuries Withnell has seen many varied spellings of its name; here are just a few from the ancient Charters of Sir Richard Hoghton: Withenhull, Withnall, Wythinhill, Wethinell, Wytenhull, Withmill, Whitnell and Wethenull.

Coppice Stile House. It must have been very cold in those bleak winters on the moors in this old farmhouse. The loaded wheelbarrow is full of peat for the fire or range. It never gave out much heat but these were hardy folk.

Mrs Sharrock with her hens at Rattenclough Farm in the 1920s. She and her family made 'picker sticks' for the looms at Hatch Farm, down Edgegate Lane. She was at one time Brinscall's oldest inhabitant.

CHAPTER TEN

Legends and Stories

PIMMS FARM

When old Gabriel Pimm died, he left a will bequeathing £4,000 to his nephew but the money was never found. As he did not believe in banks it is supposed that he hid it somewhere about the old farm and as paper money was very rare in those days, it would probably have been in gold. People claim to have seen him searching for it. The last time he was seen, a spiritual medium was brought in to investigate. After spending some time among the old ruins he said 'There is no doubt but that the money is still there and as old Gabriel never disclosed where he hid it, his spirit is still earth bound and he will continue to haunt these old ruins until it is found and returned to its rightful owner.'

MOSSCROP FARM

An old pedlar woman who used to pedal her wares around to those old farm houses on Withnell moors was found dead on Christmas morning in the farmyard at Mosscrop farm. She was found frozen to death in the snow. Many people claim to have seen her wandering around the old farm ruins.

ROCK VILLA

Just before my time there lived at Rock Villa a Curate and his wife. They did not get on well together and were always quarrelling. One night their neighbours heard them having a violent quarrel. The morning after the curate went to catch a train at Withnell station. When he got there he realised he had forgotten something and went back home for it.

When he reached home he found his wife lying on the kitchen floor, dead, with her throat cut. An inquiry was held and the verdict of suicide was returned but the neighbours formed their own conclusions.

Since then the place has been haunted. The apparition appears in many forms and I know many people who claim to have seen it. I will quote just one:

About 1893 it was the practice for my Grandfather and Grandmother to take the old horse and cart to Blackburn to 'buy in'. It was just before Christmas and they went to Blackburn on a Saturday. They arrived back at the Hare and Hounds Inn about eleven-o-clock at night, my Grandfather liked a glass of rum so stopped the horse there and went inside for a glass of hot rum and one for my Grandmother who remained seated in the front of the cart.

Then they set off on their journey home. It was a bright moonlit night. As they were passing Rock Villa three white geese suddenly appeared in the road just in front of the horse's head. As the farmers round about all kept geese you might say 'there is nothing strange about that' but there was something strange about it, all the geese were without their heads or necks yet they gobbled, gobbled, gobbled all the way as they walked in front. When they got to the quarry smithy at the top of the road they disappeared just as mysteriously as they had appeared. It might have been that tot of rum but you must form your own conclusions. That is how I heard the story many times after that.

HOLLINSHEAD HALL

> *But had I wist before I kissed*
> *That love had been so ill to win*
> *I'd locked my heart in a case of gold,*
> *And pinned it with a silver pin.*

It would be very strange if an old mansion such as this, with its old wishing well, should rise, flourish for a few centuries, then sink into oblivion without leaving some interesting legends behind.

When I was a youth I knew an old man who was born and bred in the Roddlesworth valley. As he was sure to know all about the locality and what it was like over a hundred years ago, and also the people who lived around here then, I went to him for information. As he knew my old grandfather very well, he was pleased to see me and to talk about those olden times. Here is one of the legends he related to me.

Many generations ago, the old man could not say how many, one of the daughters of the Hollinshead family became enamoured of a young man who lived at the lower end of the Roddlesworth valley. She used to meet him clandestinely and for a blind, when she set out to meet him, she always took with her an old collie dog named Nell on the pretence she was taking it for a walk.

Her father became suspicious of these constant walks and made certain enquiries. One evening, after one of these

A 19th century engraving of Hollinshead Hall.
A much larger house once stood on the site, as well as a farmhouse of considerable size with barns, outbuildings and stabling for 30 horses.

walks, he was waiting for her return. He asked her where she had been.

'Oh,' she replied, 'I have been with Nell.'

'Then you will go with Nell no more,' and in his temper he took the old dog out into the woods and destroyed it.

After that he kept a careful watch on his daughter. The young man, finding his love came no more to meet him, lost all hope and eventually hanged himself on a tree close by the place where they went to meet.

When the daughter heard of the fate of her lover, she became despondent and this, together with the loss of her favourite dog, made her fret, and eventually she pined away and died. She was her father's favourite daughter, and her death affected him so much that, although he lived to a good old age, like the king who lost his son in the wreck of the 'White Ship', he never smiled again.

At the lower end of the Roddlesworth valley, just behind the *Hare and Hounds Inn* at Abbey Village there is a place known as Engine Bottoms; here, before the reservoirs were made, the River Roddlesworth ran its uninterrupted course. It was spanned here by an old stone bridge. It was on this bridge that the lovers used to meet.

That old stone bridge was washed away more than a hundred years ago. It was replaced by a single plank bridge with a single handrail; then that bridge became derelict with the passing of the years, and about 40 years ago it was dismantled and a more modern bridge was erected in its place. This bridge still stands today. By the way, the river Roddlesworth is more popularly known as Rocky Brook.

It is said that the lovers still meet on this bridge as of old, old Nell sitting alone at one end to warn her mistress of the approach of a third party. That is the reason given why anyone approaching the bridge, from either end, has never seen them, but there is a cottage close by, the former tenants of which claim to have seen them when there has been a clear moonlit night, old Nell sitting at one end to warn her mistress of any danger.

Engine Bottoms, by the old stone bridge over the River Roddlesworth and where the lovers used to meet.

The reliance to be placed on this legend I must leave to your own judgement. I can only state what the old gentleman told me. He also told me many interesting stories of the locality and people who lived here over a hundred years ago.

Richard Robinson, Brinscall

22 December 1957

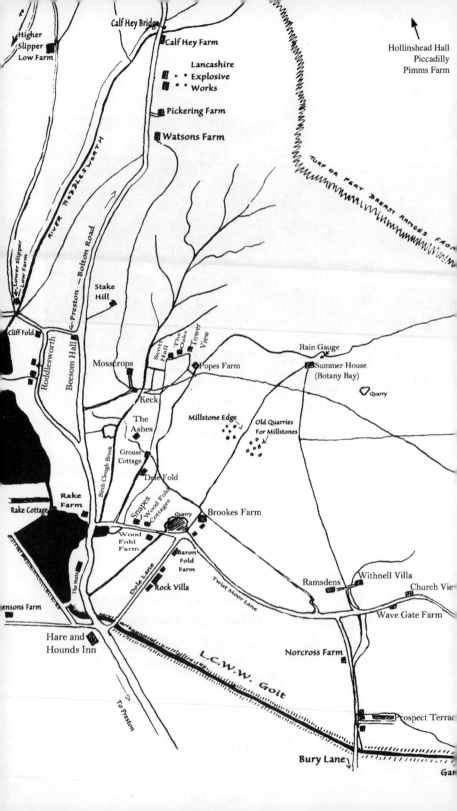

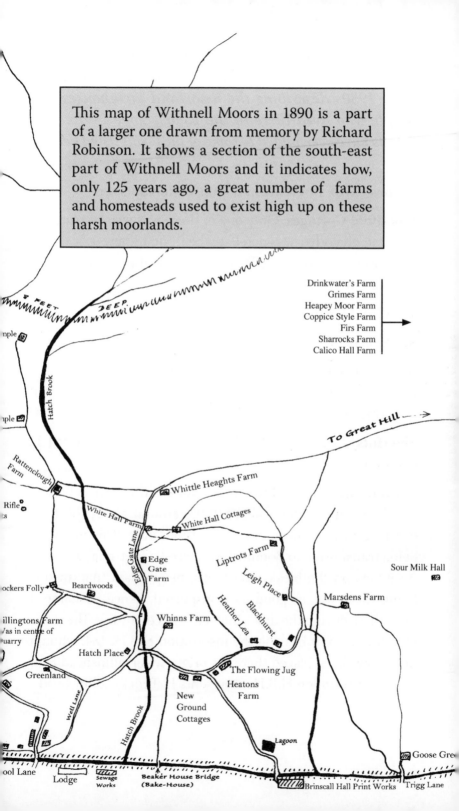

This map of Withnell Moors in 1890 is a part of a larger one drawn from memory by Richard Robinson. It shows a section of the south-east part of Withnell Moors and it indicates how, only 125 years ago, a great number of farms and homesteads used to exist high up on these harsh moorlands.

Drinkwater's Farm
Grimes Farm
Heapey Moor Farm
Coppice Style Farm
Firs Farm
Sharrocks Farm
Calico Hall Farm →

To Great Hill →

8 FEET DEEP.

Hatch Brook

Rattenclough Farm

Rifle
...es

...mple

...ool Lane

Whittle Heaghts Farm

White Hall Farm

White Hall Cottages

Edge Gate Lane

Liptrots Farm

Leigh Place

Sour Milk Hall

...ockers Folly

Beardwoods

Edge Gate Farm

Marsdens Farm

Blackhurst

Heather Lea

...illingtons Farm
...as in centre of
...uarry

Whinns Farm

Hatch Place

Greenland

Well Lane

Hatch Brook

New Ground Cottages

The Flowing Jug

Heatons Farm

Lagoon

Goose Gree...

Lodge

Sewage Works

Beaker House Bridge (Bake-House)

Brinscall Hall Print Works

Trigg Lane

The following list of buildings and the preceding map were written and drawn by Richard Robinson in the early 1950s describing the moorland farmhouses and people who lived there in the 1890s. Some 1891 census details have been added to some of the farms listed here.

Snapes Farm: Mr William Bolton, cotton Spinner.

Woodfold Cottages: Only one of these was ever tenanted in my time, the other was derelict when I first knew it. It was in this cottage where Lizzie Wain lived, one of the characters in my story of The Style.

Woodfold Farm: Mr John Duxbury, farmer.

Rake Farm: Mr Richard Marsden. (Dick O' Dolly's) Farmer.

Brooks Farm: Mr Richard Cookson. 1891 Census and Ordnance survey maps show as Hillock. Mr Cookson listed as Farmer/Labourer.

The Huts: Two families lived here. Between them they had 32 children.

The Summer House: The correct name of this farm is Botany Bay Farm. It was built about 1805, around about the time of the industrial revolution when thousands of people were being transported to Botany Bay, Australia for trivial offences. As it was on the bleak moorlands, people said that anyone living there was as good as transported, hence its name. I lived there during the first nineteen years of my life. The stone over the window bearing the inscription H.B.H. 1843 should never have been placed there. Its origin was Hollinshead Hall and the inscription H.B.H. represents H. Brock-Hollinshead.

Ramsdens Farm: Mr Robert Driver, quarryman.

Withnell Villa: Built in 1888 by Job Parkinson. On the ground where the villa now stands once stood an old farmhouse. (This farm was called Richmonds farm) I do not know its name nor do I remember ever having seen it. Just about the turn of the Century Mr Parkinson began to brew beer here. He gave a barrel of this beer to the Conservative club, just opened, and to all the public houses in the district. Although it was brewed from the finest materials, no one seemed to like it and the brewery failed and closed down. Before the brewery began, in the top corner of the ground was a large wooden hut about 18 feet square. This belonged to a Christian sect called the Christadelphians. Several Withnell families were members of the sect, the most prominent being Mr Frank Moss and family. Mr Moss was steward to Mr W.B. Park of Ollerton Hall, the owner of Abbey mill and village and all the Withnell moorlands, also the greater part of Tockholes including the old cotton mill. The Christadelphians sect does not believe in infant baptism. Hanging inside the roof of the hut was a large bath in which the followers were baptised when they came of age. When Mr Parkinson began to brew beer he purchased this hut and contents and the bath was then used for storing ingredients from which the beer is made. Which was the most useful purpose it served, you may judge for yourself.

Wave Gate Farm: Mr W. Warburton. The late Mr William Rossall and his mother lived here for many years. They left about 1900.

Popes Farm: It is now just a heap of stones by the brook side. On the Ordnance survey map it is shown as stepping stones.

Popes Farm

It was the only thatched farm house on the moors that I can recall and it was here that James Grant brought his newly-married wife, Mary in 1806 and in the May of that year their son David was born, who is the chief character, hero and benefactor of my story, The Stile. From 1898 we took over this farm. We never kept any cattle there except for a few young stirks, but we gathered the hay from the meadows and stored it in the old barn. The old fireplace with its old-fashioned Cornish (mantelpiece) and the old stairs still stood, also the room where David was born. I also knew the place where the handloom was worked that paid for David's schooling. The shippon had three double boosts (stalls) and a single one at the far end. It was here that David's pony, Jenny was stabled, and in the range just in front was where David found his mother dead. In my younger days I spent hundreds of hours around the old house, and now, looking back after all these years I remember finding many proofs that David Grant was born here and did spend his youth in that old farm house.

Dale Fold Farm: Mr John Miller, farmer. Now in ruins. This was the farm where farmer Brooks and his wife lived, two other characters in The Stile.

Grouse Cottage: Mr Joseph Snape, cotton spinner. (Joe Cragg). This building still stands.

The Ashes: (Recorded as Aushaws in 1891 Census) Mr R. Fazackerly, fireman at print works. This farm has two cottages attached. It was called the Ashes because, there and all along

Dale Fold Farm

Grouse Cottage

the 'Birch Clough Brook' for some distance grew hundreds of Mountain Ash trees. These were always a great blaze of colour in the autumn as they still are today. The local name for these trees is Wicken Berry but their real name is Rowan Tree and is Scottish in origin.

Tower View Farm: Doctor Thomas Nowell, stone quarryman. Many members of this family still live in Withnell. Mrs. Knowles, another character in The Stile lived here.

The Oaks Farm: Mr Stephen Miller, general labourer and farmer.

Scott Hall Farm: Mr Thomas Gregory, farmer and cotton weaver.

Besom Hall Farm: Mr.Robert Bateson, stone quarryman.

This farm house stood on the left hand side of the main Preston to Bolton road, exactly one mile nearer Bolton than the Hare and Hounds. You could enter the living kitchen from the level of the road, and the bedrooms were in the storeys overhead. The house was built on the road embankment and underneath the kitchen was another storey which contained the shippon, stable and pig sty.

Lower Roddlesworth Farm: Mr Thomas Bolton, farmer.

Middle Roddlesworth Farm: This was never tenanted in my time and only a long barn still stood, and here I must reflect awhile and reveal some of the mysteries connected with it. Was it once part of an old abbey? And from which the village gets its name. In 1901 a new schoolmaster came to Abbey Village by name Mr W.H. Griffiths. In passing let me say that he was one of the finest men who ever lived in the village. He was interested in local history and folk lore and he soon began to investigate and search for evidence as to why the place was called Abbey Village. Someone told him that I was born in the village and that I too was interested in history, both nationally and local. He came to see me and he asked me if I had any date or other evidence that could be useful for investigating the origin of the name Abbey Village. I told him I had heard many rumours about the old barn called Middle Roddlesworth Farm. We decided to investigate. We spent many evenings and weekends at that old building and all the land surrounding it, and, in brief, this is what we found. The old windows in that barn had been walled up but all the doors and windows that we found were arched in 'Gothic style' and in one place there were unmistakable signs that it could have been a place where an alter once stood. We examined all the

119

land between there and the reservoirs and we found many little piles of stones that looked like they had once been the foundations of buildings. We came to Halliwell Fold Bridge. Mr Griffiths had already found out that the place had once been known as 'Holy Well Fold'. We continued our search and found many interesting things and we came to the conclusion that it was possible that this had once been the site of some old Abbey or Monastery, but that was only our theory, and under no circumstances must it be accepted as proof that Abbey Village got its name from here. It is only just a fanciful theory and must be considered as that and nothing more.

Higher Roddlesworth Farm: Mr Thomas Moss, farmer. It was Mr Moss who played an unwilling part in the escapade that led to the Hollinshead family to leave the district. Mr Moss, when a very old man, confirmed the story to me, himself.

Cliff Fold Farm: Mr Eli Smith, cattle dealer.

Keck Farm: Mr William Rowley. It was at this farm that Genevieve Gordon lived, one of the chief characters in my book. It was in a little hollow just at the bottom of the mead, close by Birch Clough Brook that David Grant rested on a memorable afternoon. Between the old Keck Farm and Scott Hall there were two fields. An old stone wall divided them and where it joined the wall that ran along the side, there was a little opening or stile. It was by this stile that David and Genevieve met, but that was a hundred and forty years ago. A public footpath still runs through that stile, but the old mountain ash that hung over the brook has now fallen down and been washed away.

Mosscrop Farm: Mr Thomas Miller, farmer.

Stake Hill Farm: Mr Robert Snape.

Birch Clough Quarry: Mr John Marsden, Jack O'Daniels. This was the quarry then in the possession of quarry master Sharp, where David Grant had his first experience at stone dressing and where Sharp knocked him down and kicked him as he laid on the floor.

Billingtons Farm: Mr Joseph Billington. This farm was pulled down by myself in 1901. It was then on the edge of the quarry and the land where it stood would now be in the centre of the quarry

Greens Farm: Mr Peter Green. Only a small part of this farm now stands, the old white washed porch and many of the buildings have been demolished. Mr Green had many sons, all connected with Brinscall Brass Band. Mr Richard Green took over the conductorship after Mr John Ainsworth, he was followed by his brother the late Mr James Green who remained as conductor until the band dissolved many years ago.

Butterworth Brow Cottages. 1891 census lists 3 cottages occupied by Mr James Bradley and family in number one. Mr Thomas Hughes and family in number two and Mr Ephraim Warburton and wife in number three.

Greenlands Farm and cottages. 1891 Census lists three dwellings. Mr Thomas Clarkson and family. Mr H.Cowburn and family and Mrs Agnes Clarkson (widow) and family plus three lodgers. All working in either the Calico print works or the Quarry.

Well Lane. 1891 Census lists three properties, again, all working in Calico print works, cotton mill, bleach works or quarry.

Hatch Farm: Mr James Sharrock. Only a few foundation stones now remain but there is still a little building there. Here pickers were once made. It is still known by the oldest villagers as the 'Picker Shop'. Pickers were made of buffalo hide and were used on cotton looms. They drove the shuttle from one end of the loom to the other. They were later made in one of the small rooms under the old Binding room. This building which stands on the corner of School Lane and Railway Road was last used as a cinema.

Beardwood Farm: Mr Thomas Eastham. This family still carry on as florists in Blackburn.

Cockers Folly: Mr Thomas Counsell.

Ratten Clough Farm: Mr W.Cotton. He removed from here to Pickering Farm when he became gamekeeper on Withnell moors.

Solomon's Temple: Mr William Rossall, born 1812, farmer.

Old Temple: Only the old barn still stood when I was a boy.

Edge Gate Farm: It has been in ruins all my life.

White Hall Farm: Mr William Barnes.

White Hall Cottages. 1891 census records Mr James Bolton, stone quarryman. There were two cottages. A public footpath still runs by both the farm and the cottages.

Whittle Heights Farm: Mr Isaac Heaton.

Ratten Clough Farm

Whins Farm: 1846 and 1896 Ordnance survey maps show this as Heatons or Heaton House Farm respectively. 1891 Census shows Mr Thomas and Martha Heys as Farmer and wife. Alice Heys, 16, daughter working in cotton mill.

Hatch Quarry

New Ground Cottages: (Five) Now only the foundations remain. 1891 Census lists six cottages and two farms all occupied at that time.

Whittle Heights Farm

New Ground Farm: Material from this farm was used in the building of the first four houses in Chapel Street in the early 1900s.

Heaton House Farm: New ground farm in 1891 census farmed by Mr John Knight, Annie his wife and four children, three working in cotton mill plus granddaughter as scholar aged 8.

Five Cottages: Now only foundations remain. Here lived Mr Gabriel Taylor, an old dry stone waller who built most of the old stone walls on Withnell moor. An old besom maker, Mr George Brindle lived here. His son Harry O' Judds carried on this occupation for many years. When he died, there passed the last of the besom makers from these moors. When the L.C.W.W. goit was made about the middle of the nineteenth century, all the cottages and farms along this route were allowed to sell beer, licence 5/- per year. The condition was that they found lodgings for the workmen. This place was called 'The Flowing Jug'.

Heather Lea: Mr Oliver Smethurst, greengrocer.

Leigh Place: 1891 census lists a Mr Robert Grundy as a stone quarryman, his wife Jane and four daughters, two working in cotton mill, one half time in mill and one scholar

Blackhurst: Mr E. Woods. He was chief steward for Mr W.B.Park. He was one of the inventors of the celluloid collars etc. Thousands of out-sized collars were stored here until it was pulled down about 1910.

Liptrot Farm: Mr James Bolton, stone quarryman.

Heather Lea

Marsdens Farm: Mr Thomas Dixon, night watchman at the print works

Goose Green: 1891 Census records a Mr Henry Hogg as a farmer, his wife Rachel and his daughter Sarah (aged 21) as an Elementary school teacher.

Just by Withnell Moors was Higher Close House farm at Stanworth, near Abbey village.

The End

ANCIENT LINEAGE OF
THE HOUSE OF HOLLINSHEAD

The seat of Henry Brock-Hollinshead, Esq. is situated about five miles to the south-west of Blackburn, in that parish, and in the township of Tockholes.

The house stands near the moor, through which passes the river Roddlesworth (or as it is sometimes termed 'the Moulder Water') and was originally very extensive, but in 1776, it was almost entirely pulled down, and re-modelled as it now stands, by an ancestor of the present owner. At the back of the building is an ancient terrace walk, leading or what was formerly called 'the Holy Spring.' Here no less than five different springs of water, after uniting together and passing through a very old carved stone, representing a lion's head, flow into a well. To this well pilgrimages were formerly made, and the water which is of a peculiar quality, is remarkable as an efficacious remedy in ophthalmic complaints.

The manor of Tockholes is stated to have been in the possession of the family of Hillinshead before 1400, but after that time, (Ist Henry IV) it was sold. In 1498 t was held by Sir Aleander Houghton. In the 17th century Chalres I (1641) it was in the possession of Nicholas Whittone; and subsequently the Hollinshead family again became proprietors.

Hugh Holynshed, or Holyns of Holyn's-head, in the lordship of Sutton, in the county of Chester, about the 25the Henry III. (1240), left a son,

Laurence Holynshed, whose second son,

Edward, married Anne, heiress of Ralph Cophurst, and was great-grandfather of

William Holynshed, who held lands in Tockholes. His son,

John Holynshed, of Sutton and Cophurst, leaft two sons, Ralph and William. From the former was descended Ralph Holinshed, of

Copurst, the Chronicler, who died ihtout issue about the year 1580. The second son,

William Holynshed, held land sin Sutton in 1434, and died in 1453. His descendant,

John Hollynshed, Esq. of Maxfield, by Ellen Parson, left eight sons and three daughters.

William Hollinshed, Esq, the eighth son, lived at Nottingham, and married Miss Raye, by whom he had twelve sons and four daughters. His fifth son,

Edward Hollinshed, Esq. married Isabella, the daughter of Charles Fitton, and left a son,

Edward Hollinshead, Esq. whose only daughter,

Emma, married Edward Brock, Esq. of Bakewell, descended from a junior branch of the family of Brock, of Upton, in Cheshire. Their grandson,

William Brock, Esq. took the name of Hollinshead on succeeding to the estates of his cousin, John Hollinshead. He died without issue in 1803, and left his estates and name to his nephew,

Laurence Brock, Esq. who thereupon took the name Hillinshead in addition to his own. He died 25th July 1835, and was succeeded by his eldest surviving son.

Henry Brock-Hollinshead, Esq. the present inheritor of Hollinshead Hall, and the representative of two families. Mr. Brock-Hollinshead, who in September 1845, married Margaret daughter of James Neveill, Esq. of Beardwood, near Blackburn, is Lord of the Manor of Tockholes, and holds the Commission of the Peace for the County of Lancaster.

Extract from *Mansions of England and Wales*
Edwin Twyercross, 1847

Archives of Lancashire County Records Office